But Still Try To Win

I0192083

1

Love Is A Gamble

Love Is A Gamble, But Still Try To Win

The Poetic Soap Opera

Paul (Phroze) Munson

poetryyoudig.com

Love Is A Gamble

Dedication

I dedicate this book to my lovely wife for hanging in there with me through it all. She is, my winning hand. I'm not throwing these cards back.

to my two beautiful daughters for pushing me to be a real life super hero.

to my mother for supporting me in everything I have ever done. I'm sure she is still doing poetry at the open mic in Heaven.

to both of my parents for speaking in front many audiences which inspired me to do the same.

to my poetic siblings for supporting me ever since they have been alive. They have always had my back.

I always dedicate my books to two of my friends "Jay "Rolla" Bennett and Brant Hudson". I am sure Rolla is working the door at that same open mic and Brant is making sure, everything is in order.

to all of my other family and friends for all of their love and support.

-Paul (Phroze) Munson

Love Is A Gamble

Love Is A Gamble, But Still Try To Win

The Poetic Soap Opera

Paul (Phroze) Munson

Not Just Alphabets Publishing

Hattiesburg, Mississippi

All Not Just Alphabets Publishing titles, Phrozen Productions, imprints and lines distributed are available at special quantity discounts for bulk purchases for sale promotion, fund raising, premiums, educational, institutional, and library use.

Printed in the U. S. A.

Library of Congress Catalog Card Number:

ISBN-13: 978-0-692-13893-9

ISBN-10: 0962138935

Cover Design by: Devie Perry

Welcome to:

The Poetic Soap Opera

Love Is A Gamble

Introduction

Love can be a gamble, but you still should not give up. We all go through different stages in relationships. You never know the final outcome until it comes. As we get older, most of us mature. Some don't but might one day. Love can drive you crazy or it can be the greatest thing that ever happened to you. It feels good at times and sometimes it hurts. One loss does not mean the love game is over. You have to keep trying. I think this book is good for adults of all ages. It is in no way a book for Children. I REPEAT. "THIS IS NOT A BOOK FOR CHILDREN." As you read this book, you should be able to relate to at least a couple of the different stages in relationships. Keep playing the cards you are dealt and enjoy the process.

It might hurt at times, but it is still worth a shot. One love.

Contents

Act I

Not All My Children 17

Act II

The Restless and Young 25

Act III

General Community Hospital 35

Act IV

Our Life to Live 41

Act V

Brian's Hope 45

Act VI

The Beautiful and Bold 51

Act VII

In Another World 57

Act VIII

Guiding Right 61

Act IX

All These Days In Our Lives 67

Act X

As The World Turns and Turns Again 71

Act XI

Hard Knocks Landing 77

Act XII

My True Passion 83

Act XIII

Too Hot, For T V But; Not Too Hot, For Me 87

Thank You 97

About The Author 99

Acknowledgements 100

Contact Information 101

Love Is A Gamble

Love Is A Gamble But, Still Try to Win

"The Poetic Soap Opera"

(All characters in this soap opera are fictional characters)

Characters:

Narrator	*Payton & Sandy*
Postman	*David & Thelma*
Tony & Michelle	*Roberto & Yolonda*
Brian & Nia	*Tommy & Tiffany*
Gary	*Michael & Carmen*
George & Veronica	*Jeremy & Shante'*
Joe & Carla	*Tyrone & Amy*

Stephon & Sophia

Love Is A Gamble

ACT I

'Not All My Children'

Love Is A Gamble

Narrator:

They were all young and ready. As they grew older; through time, they learned that relationships have ups and downs, but they never did give up. They kept on playing the cards they were dealt. It was always a part of their journey to get them where they are now and where they are going. Life deals out many relationships. Don't give up. You get what your heart truly desires and sometimes you may even desire something a lot better than the situation you are in.

{Payton sits in his dorm room on the edge of his bed all alone as he keeps glancing at the mirror hanging on the closet door}

Payton:

I am not supposed to feel like this. It is not supposed to be me feeling this type of way, but I guess it happens when you see someone almost every day. I'm supposed to be this; "feeling great single man," but sometimes it feels like I was dealt a bad hand. I mean, what happened? Has my plan backfired? She said she is ready to retire, from so many mixed up emotions. She says she is ready for devotion.

It is really kind of hard to explain. If I lose this woman, there is only myself to blame. My plan is to not have a girlfriend, and because of this, she thinks the relationship we have should end. I wish she would give it another spin, but she still says, "she wants a boyfriend". She believes that together, we can win. I told her, "I am sorry, but I just can not bend." At the time, "I don't want a girlfriend", and it seems like she blew in the wind. Now, my da*n feelings are hurt, and she is missed, but in my plan, "I am not supposed to feel like this"!

I have my whole life ahead of me. I just don't want to rush into anything. I also don't want to commit to commitment. I just wish she felt the same. I just want to take it slow. There may even be a chance that things can change but, she doesn't have time to wait and see. I wish we could at least try to stay friends instead of breaking up what we have together. Either way, someone ends up with a broken heart. I probably wouldn't feel this way if I hadn't been in that one relationship before, that broke my heart. I was younger and way ahead of my time. I'm not sure. I think it was infatuation. I still remember the last thing I said to her...

{Payton stands up and paces back and forth in the dorm room as he reminisces}

Payton:

I thought I loved you, and my love was true. Sometimes, I felt "blue" and I didn't know what to do. Then you came to mind, and I would start feeling just fine. I feel better now. I do not know how, but I do. I guess it was because I thought I loved you. When I was younger in my youth, I could not stop thinking about you. I would write your name on my hands, arms, books, and folders. I wrote it on my desks, shoes, and book covers. I wanted to let the whole world know. Like a clown, I would put on a show. I did whatever you asked of me, because you had the key, to my heart as they say. I thought about you every day, and night. My school work was never right, because I would not listen to the teacher. I thought you were really a keeper. I was always thinking of you. Once, I told my mother that I had the flu, just so I could stay home from school. Of course, you were sick and staying home too. Everyone in my house was mad at me. All we had was a land line and I stayed on the phone with you constantly.

I didn't know what love was, but I was curious. I took everything you said, serious. Even when you lied to me, I believed. I never thought of you to have "tricks up your sleeve" but I see I was wrong, and we ended what I thought would last long. I don't know if it was lust or love for me. Whatever it was, your eyes couldn't seem to see.

What you had, you eventually lost. In the long run, it will cost, and you will wish I was still there. Now, I have started to care, for another young lady that you do not know. If you told me you loved me now, I would not hesitate to show, you the door. The fact is that; you and I, are no more.

A "young player," has to think this thing out. I am going to take my time. I might feel different later in life, but this is me right now. I'm only 20 years old and I still want to have fun. As a matter of fact, I forgot I was going to the club tonight. I'm a "turn up" tonight and, see what I can pull...

[Club Scene]

{Payton is in the club "holding up the wall" talking to his friends}

Payton:

Man, I'm fina try to "pull" this female, and if I don't, oh well. At least, I tried. My feelings, I will not let hide. I want her on my every side. If I get her, I will take much pride. I wish I could explain to her that eventually I want her on my team. I want to bring reality to her best dreams. I want her to feel this excitement that I feel. I am going to try to pull her, for real. I mean, she is "fine as all get out". I just hope I say the right things with my mouth. I have no choice but to "pull" her, like it is "tug of war". Out of all the females in here, she is the "super star".

I think, "I'm in loooove". I think she already has me "spruuuung." Through her dress, it looks like she has on a thooooong. I know that is beside the point; plus, I could be wrooooong. I'm telling you, "this girl is so preeetty." If she gives me a chance, I'll stop being so fliiiirty. Well, I'm fina go ahead and bust my move. Soon as I got ready to say something, she started kissing some dude. I just walked on by like I didn't even see them two. I mean; he*l, what would you do?

1 of the friends:

I still would have tried to holla. She just that "bad". I wouldn't give a d*mn.

Payton:

Yea, you say that, but I didn't want any problems. I know that you say that you don't give a crap, but I do. You might welcome the challenge, but I have enough sense to understand that there are" plenty more fish in the sea and even more in the ocean". Plus, she may have been a shark, or a sting ray. Sometimes, it is best to just stay in the boat for the ride. Hold up. Hold up. Excuse me player, but another "bad one" just walked by and she was looking right at me! I'm fina go hollla. Watch ya boy go to work.

{Payton walks up to her with all the "swag "he has. His confidence is through the roof.}

Payton:

Young lady, can I talk to you? First; of all, "how do you do"? I will not take up too much of your time. Unlike these other dudes, I don't have memorized lines, trying to make you "fall head over hills". I just want to let you know how I feel.

You are a beautiful young lady. I can see that you are different and just maybe, you will find the time to give me a chance. When I first saw you, it was at a glance. Then I took another look that was stronger. This is when my whole body started to hunger, just to meet someone with such beauty and such grace. I had to come and speak to you face to face.

Well, I don't want to hold you too long. I am not asking for your number, but you can call me at home. Whenever you get some time, just call me on my line. With that being said, "I'll let you be on your way". When I do hear from you again, I know it will make my day. If you want to call tonight, I'll be at home, and we can continue this conversation over the telephone.

Sandy:

O. K., I'll take your number because I usually don't give out my number to guys. I won't lie. I used to even give out the wrong number until a guy said, "let me call you right quick so you will have my number". I should have known that was a set up, but anyway, you didn't even ask for my number, so I might go ahead and give you a chance. Plus, you are kind of cute.

Payton:

Well, I look forward to hearing from you and I am glad I didn't ask for the number because I almost did. Thank God that I didn't. Well anyway, I'm sure I'll see you again before the club closes. Don't let me hold you up. Enjoy the rest of your night.

{Later that night which is early in the morning, Sandy surprises Payton with a phone call. They talk for a little while and then she asked Payton this...}

Sandy:

So, Payton, why don't you have a woman?

Payton:

See, I am not looking for a relationship, and if I end up in one, that will really be a "trip." I hope my woman's personality doesn't flip, and I hope her attitude doesn't click and if I am getting ahead of myself, tell me to quit. Let me explain this script.

Sit back and try to understand. I am a young, single man. I am not trying to rush. I am what I am. I'm really trying to do all that I can. I'm not ready to walk hand and hand, and so far, I have stuck to the plan.

I would love to have a lady friend in my life. One day, I wouldn't mind having a wife, even though being young and single is, pretty nice. If I could live my life again, I would live it twice. I want my woman to help me feel high as a kite. I aim to please, so I hope she really likes. I think I need a relationship in my life. Then again, I might not be right.

See, my girlfriend might end up being a "thot". She might wait till we are in public and then try "blow up the spot". I might need to leave, and she might not want me to go. Behind my back, she might go "down low". Relationships, I really do not know. She might try to hold me down when I am trying to grow. When I speed up, she might want me to go slow. Trying to get to the top, she might try to keep me low. She might try to hold me back when I am trying to go. I'm just not really looking for a relationship, but who knows what the future may hold in it.

I mean, I am just not looking for a girlfriend, but I cain't lie. I wouldn't mind having one again. I would not mind being held by a lady. I can be a "born again virgin" or help her practice making babies. I am not trying to give you any hints, but with a female is how I want my time spent. I wouldn't mind hearing, "I love you," but only if that statement is true.

I am not looking for a lady or a wife. I just want someone special in my life. I want someone that can make me laugh. I want someone that will "have my back." Sometimes, I want a lady's point of view. I only want one point, not many or a few. I want her to have patience with my mind; and stay positive and try not to fall behind. Physically, she needs to be neat and clean. Her personality needs to be nice and not mean. I am not looking for a girlfriend. 'Right now, I am really just looking for a friend.

Sandy:

Well, we just met. I didn't know you were going to say that much though and, you are confusing me just a little bit. You are not looking for a girlfriend, but you wouldn't mind having one? Well, I am not looking for a boyfriend at all, right now. Is that something you can deal with?

Payton:

I respect that. I know we are both just "doing our thang." I was just saying. I may have said too much though, huh?

Sandy:

No, you good. I just wanted to be straight up. I don't have time for reading between the lines. This way, everyone knows exactly what is going on. Conversation always helps the situation.

Payton:

You not like these other females. Other females figure you just supposed to already know what they are thinking. I really like that. We can move on without wondering, ya dig.

ACT II

'The Restless and The Young'

{Scene opens up in the post office. David waits in line to talk to the post office worker.}

David:

Mr. Postman, can you help me, please? I don't know if my letters have been received. I have mailed off two or three, but there was no return and that, I don't believe. I don't mean to be rude but, "Give me the da*n key!" I don't mean to go crazy but why haven't my letters been received?! Mr. Postman, can you help me please, and don't tell me that she received my letter, because I will choke someone like a "too little turtle neck sweater"! Mr. Postman, don't run me hot like "Texas summer time weather"! Tell me where my da*n mail is, and I will feel better! Are you letting my mail float around like a feather?! Mr. Postman don't make me jump you like checkers! Now Mr. Postman, can you help me please? I paid for my stamp and my da*n envelope! I think you are taking my mail for a joke! I want that woman to read what I wrote! I'm getting ready to go "postal" in here because I cain't cope! Mr. Postman, I know you don't want your body in the river like a float! You've misplaced letters, poems, and p. s. notes, and Mr. Postman, I just want you to help me please.

Maybe it is true that she just hasn't written me back, but I need your help to find out if this is a fact. There is no use of writing again since she hasn't written back. Excuse me but deep inside, someone should be slapped, but right now, I will not worry about that. Mr. Postman, I just want to know where my letters are at. (crying) So Mr. Postman, can you help me please?

Postman:

Man, you something crazy! I am going to have to ask you to leave or I will call for some help to escort you, away from this property! I have no reason to keep any of your mail! I don't know you and I don't know that woman that is driving you crazy!

David:

I'm sorry but a part of me hopes she didn't even receive any of the mail. I mean, I have been trying too hard and moving way too fast. I'm sorry. I'll be leaving sir.

{David gets back in his car and proceeds to head home. He turns the radio down and starts to talk to himself still feeling kind of down}

Did I send the letter too late or too soon? Have you ever held in what you had to say inside? Have you ever had a little too much pride, and by the time you brought it up, everything had died? How many more good women will I let get by?

We are just friends today. I tend to stand in my own way. She shined on me like the opposite of shade. I wish she was more than a friend, o.k. She was so pleasant and desirable. I wanted to offer her full coverage, not just liable. I should have told her way before now, but my "ole scary" self, seemed to not know how. I kept my thoughts to myself when they should have been loud! In my mind, I thought I had her with no doubt.

I wrote that last letter too let her know how I finally feel. I folded it up, put it in the envelope, and licked it to seal. With those words that I mailed, I had to let my true feelings spill. I called the very next day and said, "how are you doing? What's the deal"? I was surprised that she answered the phone because I kept getting the answering service. The letter wasn't there yet. She answered the phone and I got nervous. I felt like a clown and she was running the circus. I couldn't help that I felt this way. It wasn't on purpose.

She really crushed me when I heard her say, that she had been busy spending time with her "bae", so I punched a hole through the wall. Then I just hung up the phone that I used to call. I have not talked to her since that very day. I never received any response in any type of way. "I hope I put the wrong address on that envelope" is what I say, but who am

I fooling? Who am I "trying to play"? I would send her this poem but I ain't sending no more sh*t! I mean; for real, I'm through trying. I quit!

Have you ever held in what you had to say inside? Have you ever had a little too much pride and by the time you brought it up, everything had died? How many more good women will I let get by? I sent that da*n letter too late and too soon. I hope it did get lost. I cain't even much lie.

{David is walking around the house. Shortly after, his phone rings. He is already frustrated and lets Thelma "have it".}

David:

You know what? Last time we talked, I called you a bit*h after I hung up the phone. You make me so sick, but I cain't leave you alone! You told me you were just being blunt, but I think you were just talking noise. I am trying to stop talking about you to my" boyz," because they get tired of hearing what might not even come true. I called you a bit*h after I hung the phone up with you, because I left you four messages on two different phone lines! I even telepathically called you with my mind, but I guess your third eye was blind. I let a week go by and I called you again. With you, is how I wanted my time to spend. I guess I must "cut for you" a whole lot. I am not trying to sweat you or hand cuff you like a cop, and I wasn't really calling you a bit*h, but you should have seen me though. I let that phone have it real, quick. I told the phone to "shut the he*l up, and I didn't want to hear sh*t"! I know I sound crazy and am too grown to be "throwing a fit". We have never been together, but it still feels like you "split" and I do apologize because I shouldn't have even called the phone a bit*h.

Thelma:

Oh, were you talking to me, with your crazy self?! I know you better just been talking to the phone because you were not talking to me like that. I ain't nobody's bit*h and if that is how you feel, don't call me no more! I don't have time to entertain anyone that even thinks about calling me out of my name. I've been meaning to talk to you about something anyway.

David:

What? What you want to talk to me about?

Thelma:

You are starting to like me too much.

{David abruptly hangs up the phone and says...}

David:

I cain't stand her a*s!

{David talks to himself again as he faces the audience.}

David:

I cain't believe she said, "I like her too much. I cain't lie. From this lady, I could not get enough, but I was shocked when she told me this line. She made my feelings in the front fall behind. I cain't lie. I liked her a whole lot. Then in so many words, she told my likes to stop. She said that she meant no harm, but I could not find her offering any kind of charm. This feeling she felt, I didn't know. If I had to choose, she is always on the front row, but now I am trying to learn to push her back. I wish this was "make believe" and not a fact. I didn't know there was a such thing as liking someone too much, but she let me know with a straight face and no bluff. She told me I took it the wrong way. I think she said that because of the expression on my face. From a phrase like this, I guess I will just have to accept, but she surely made a brother's heart feel upset.

I didn't know how to react to this statement. No one ever told me something like that. I was some what in shock. I was trying too hard and not getting any results. I think that is one definition of insanity. It got to a point to where she didn't even want to hear my voice anymore.

{David calls Thelma later in the day. Thelma has been wanting to tell him a thing or two.}

Thelma:

Hello. Really? Don't ever call my ph*cking number again and I won't call you!

{Thelma hangs the phone up in David's face. "I said she just wanted to say a thing or two..."}

David:

I called this lady whose name I will not say. I was calling for general conversation and to see if she had a good day. She answered the phone with a polite, "hello". She heard my voice and started to "blow"! She heard rumors through one ear but didn't let them fall out the other. The rumors she heard made her wonder. She told me what they were one by one. When I answered back, the conversation was done.

She didn't believe a word that I said. She just let the rumors marinate in her head. She told me, "don't call me and I won't call you". I asked if she was sure about what she wanted to do. She replied, "yes" so I guess, I will no longer call this female bringing me so much stress.

{David is not supposed to call anymore but, he had to call one last time. He had a gut feeling about something that he never brought up and he just wants to get it off his chest.}

Thelma:

Hello. Hello. Are you really calling me again? I thought I made myself clear!

David:

Don't worry. This is my last time calling you, for real. I just wanted to let you know that, I can tell, that you had been "kicking it" with another dude, but you know me, "it's cool". Go ahead and kick it with the other dude. There is no reason for me to get rude. Never say never, but never again will I just assume. I could tell something was fishy. I could smell the fumes. You used to shine on me before you started throwing shade. We were "kicking it tough". Then, you started to fade. I don't know if I will ever understand pretty women ways, but I know how it goes, so it is really o.k.

If I am not the groom at your wedding, I am going to try to put your eye out when I throw my rice. Oh, I forgot, "I'm not supposed to put up a fight". I can tell because the conversation is short and boring. I am surprised that you are not snoring. I know you are doing it on purpose. This, I am knowing. I know you are ready for me to be going.

Deep inside, I want to "act a donkey"! I want to "act a mule" but I forgot that I said, "everything is cool". I just want to be stubborn like "hard head kids in school". I could tell there was another dude, because you had left a trail of clues. You know da*n well, you are not supposed to "kick it" with another dude! I'm just serious. I mean, I'm just playing. Whatever you do is cool.

Thelma:

Are you finished?

David:

Yes, I guess.

Thelma:

First, of all, you are not my man! Secondly, I told yo a*s that I had a "bae"! I know we hang out and "kick it" but we were just friends. I didn't know you were feeling some type of way. I have never cared about you hanging out with other females because we are not together. I apologize if I gave you that vibe. That was not my intentions. You were like a crazy brother to me. You real crazy though!

David:

O. K., o.k. I've heard that so many times; not the crazy part but the "like a brother" part. I've heard it more times than I wanted to. At least, I know now, though. I don't have to waste too much energy thinking in the wrong direction. I need to learn to just let life just become. Some-times it is a good thing that things don't work out the way you think you want them to. I remember a guy that I worked with at the temp service. He told me a story that happened to him back in the day. Listen to what he said:

{Thelma hangs the phone up, but David is still talking. He hasn't realized she hung it up}

Roses really smell like "boo boo". I'm not "Outkast" but roses really do, when you listen to the story I am about to tell you. The rose was red, but the violence made me feel "blue". I went to work early that day. At 11:00 a.m., I took my first break. I am a faithful worker too. I am never late. I loved my woman with a passion. There was no hate. I bought her a rose like it was our first date. I was going to surprise my baby. I couldn't wait, and to my surprise, she was laid up with some "jail bait". I won't repeat my words, but they were not very great.

She had a young stud. He was only 19. Lord knows, I wish this was a dream, but it wasn't. It had become my reality. I was ready to take him out like a casualty. Mr. 19 was one of her fellow co-worker employees. They must have really been into it too because at the door, no one heard the keys. We fought for a while before I finished whooping his tail. When I kicked him out the door, he fell, like geronimooooooo, down the stairs. I went to jail for a week and a half. Of course, my lady is gone now if you must ask. I've "touched down," single, and available again. That rose I bought smelled like, "boo boo" and that is the end.

That's a trip ain't it...hello...hello...hello...

{David presses the phone hang up button as hard as he can and yells...}

I promise I cain't stand her a*s!...

Love Is A Gamble

ACT III

'General Community Hospital'

Narrator:

He cain't wait for her to visit again. He really hates for their visits to see an end. When she would "hit him in the d. m," or give him a telephone call, he would start blushing and his mouth falls. His eyes popped completely out. To her house, he is ready to take the route. His heart starts beating at a faster pace. To see her, time he doesn't waste. Her visits make him jump up and down. Her visits make him do flips and spin around. They make him stomp his feet and clap his hands. She is the lady visiting this man. He is ready to show her a good time. Her absence is the reason for this rhyme.

{Tony is in the mirror talking to himself as he gets dressed for tonight}

Tony:

"I got to get right". I got to get over to this barber shop and get "chopped up". I "gotta" get my shirt out of the cleaners too. Pablo already got my shoes shinning like a diamond. Speaking of diamond, "let me d. m. mine.

I cain't wait to see you again. I mean, just how long has it been? I'm sorry, who am I to question time, but when I see you again, that moment will be divine. If you think about it, everything is yesterday, so that leaves us to go with today. Tomorrow might come also. I want to see you again is all I know. I really "dig your personality. I hope my thoughts become my reality.

You are one with such humbleness and grace. I look forward to the day we come face to face. I love that you put business before pleasure. Once our paths cross again; that moment I will treasure. I have always known you to have a positive attitude. "I can't wait to see you" is the headline news! There is a bulletin going out across the universe. Will I find you or will you find me first?

Who really knows if we will even meet again? If we do, I hope that meeting never ends. The Lord knows I really like you a whole lot. When I see you; my mouth, drops! My eyes pop completely out of socket! You have the key to my heart, but you won't unlock it! My tongue falls to the floor! It is you that I go crazy for! I must cool down because I'm getting "red hot". My feelings, I can not seem to stop. I just cain't wait to see you again.

I will tell the world I love you but will not say your name, because if I don't get the right response, I only have myself to blame. I'm just not the type of man that is brought to shame. Deep inside, I want you to be my "main." A relationship with you is what I want to claim. With you on my team, I make the "hall of fame". You keep me feeling high like a "D. F. W. airplane". You keep me on track like a freight train. When I am down and out, you pick me up like a crane.

I love you but can not say your name, because you might tell me that my feelings are lame. I should give up, but I keep trying again and again (pronounced a gain and a gain). You are the brace that heals my sprains. I stay hot for you like a gas stove bringing flame. You are the picture and I'm just asking if I can come inside the frame. With you, I am vibrant. Without you, I am plain. To love me back shouldn't be a strain. I will tell the world I love you but will not say your name.

I don't know what it will take. I need to stop "sweating you". I need to move on. You know all of this but don't respond back to me. Am I wasting my time or what? You know what...

I'm through waiting on you. I know you are saying, "thank you" and probably "rolling your eyes," but hear me out one last time. I've tried, and I've tried. I would try even harder, but I keep getting shot down. I get tired of "picking my face up off the ground." You've told me time and time again, not to jump to conclusions. Many times, I see you, but it turns out to be an illusion. I keep trying to get you out of my thoughts because they end up in confusion. I get nervous like I don't know what "the h*ll" I'm doing. I throw clues here and there. You turn your head, miss the catch, and act as if you don't care.

Life is life, so I guess it is fair. You are a diamond in the rough.

Baby, you are rare, and I'm finally starting to accept that you might not be mine. I'm through waiting on you but I might be lying (pronounced line). Da*n woman, "you fine!" Why do you insist on making me wait in line? Well, don't answer that question. I know that I am finally learning my lesson.

I need a guarantee instead of just hoping and guessing. I'm just gone leave it in God's hands and start resting. My energy will start going towards what benefits me. Sitting up in here wishing I could have you brings me misery. All I know is that I am through waiting on you, even though deep in my heart, I don't want to.

{Tony reads his message that just came from Michelle.}

Michelle:

I just don't want to move too fast. I told myself that I would take my time before I made big decisions like that again. I just recently got out of a relationship that was not very healthy for me. I just don't want to get hurt again. I had me a "rough neck" and that was a little too rough for me.

{Tony is a poet. He sits down and writes this piece.}

Tony:

She came to be with me but left to get away from me. I was too hot for her like, "sizzling." I stayed too "dirty" for her like chitterlings. She tried to hang around like ear rings. She followed, and I was leading. I broke her heart like a busted vein that is bleeding. I wasn't trying to break her heart. I was just being myself from the start. What was once sweet is now tart. She was a beautiful lady. She was a star. She looked good at church or at the bar.

She saw how I was and realized that I wasn't ready for change.

She hoped my situation would rearrange. Maybe, we were not supposed to be together, so no one gets the blame. I don't apologize for any of my actions. I am not ashamed. I only do what I do to maintain. I never take any glory in "the game." I'm not just riding band wagons or trains. For the wrong reasons, I never wanted to end up in the wrong "hall of fame." I guess I wasn't "Godly" enough for her to have faith in me like a "mustard grain."

If I don't change for myself, the change is lame. She has a man now is what she claims. For all I know, she has probably always had that main (man). That's cool though because I never lock down like chains. She wasn't ready for someone with book and street brains. I know someone feels me. My situation is not that strange. She missed the target in which she was trying to take aim. She flew in on a round trip airplane. She couldn't understand my life. She wanted me to explain.

She said my life was "Rated R" and she didn't want my bad habits to leave a stain. She got tired of me spending so much time with "Ms. Jane". She really missed out when she had so much to gain. She thought I would break her five heart beats like "Eddie Cane." My life was too fast for her. She wanted to put the stopper in my drain.

My ways were foreign to her like a trip to the, "Ukraine". We were finally in the same photograph, but she stepped out of the frame. Stressful thoughts about me made her feel so much pain. Her feelings for me, "hit the ground" like rain. She wanted me to get out of her brain. She felt me through her cells and veins. She is gone now so there is no reason to ever say her name. She came to be with me but left to get away from me. I was too hot for her. I was hot like "sizzling", ya dig.

ACT IV

'Our Life to Live'

{Roberto calls Yolonda}

Roberto:

It was good hearing your voice tonight. I called right before I got ready to turn off the lights. Now that I heard your voice, I can sleep tight. Hearing your voice is the reason I must write. We did not talk long at all. The conversation was short and not tall. I got home from work and said to myself that, I must call. I am holding on to you like you are about to fall.

Hearing your voice helps me get through the week. Your voice reminds me to stay humble and meek. To your place or mine, we always creep. You need to be a resident on my street. It is your voice that I took to bed. I pray to the Lord that you stay in my head. Not seeing you, I always dread. I was really blessed to hear the words you said. It was so good hearing your voice tonight.

Yolonda:

I am actually glad you called. I've been thinking about you all day. I knew you were at work and I didn't want to bother you, so I was glad when the caller i.d. read your name.

Roberto:

I've been meaning to speak with you about something for the last couple of weeks.

Yolonda:

What's wrong? What happened? What are you trying to tell me?

Roberto:

Will you be quiet baby and just listen.

Yolonda:

O. K. "papi." I'm listening.

Roberto:

Will you be my lady? I want yes or no, not maybe. I really want you to be my number one. Will you take this chance with my parents' son? I want you on my team. I want to keep seeing you in my dreams. I want you to know that; on me, you can depend on. You know I love hearing your sweet voice on the telephone. I promise to take care of you. Every word I write is so true. I will always treat you with respect. I will massage you to help give you rest. You will be treated as a queen. I just want you to allow me to be your king. Will you be my lady? I want yes or no, not maybe.

Because, if you asked me to be your man; more than likely, I would respond "I can." You would have everything that you desire. You are "hot" baby like fire. I am your sun and you are my moon. Just imagine being the bride and I being the groom. If you asked me to be your man, your thoughts I would try to understand.

Your love, I would try to feel. I would be your "Black Panther or Super Man of Steel." I will be your "any and everything." I would try to bring reality to your best dreams. I will massage you to help make you feel good. I want to be together like neighbor and hood. I want to hold you like the ink in a ball point pen. I am "9" but with you, I make "10"

My goal would be to make you happy every day. Together is how I would want us to stay. Anything you want, I would try to make sure you have. It will make me happy to see you laugh. I will try to make sure you have all the finer things in life, simply because, you are my "want to be wife." If you asked me to be your man; more than likely, I would respond,

43

"I can."

Yolonda:

"Oh papi", I'm really enjoying this ride. You are everything I dreamed of in a man. I just want to make sure because this is a big step. I've already been thinking about it a whole lot, though. Let me sleep on it, "papi." Now, you get some sleep, too and I will call you first thing in the morning.

ACT V

'Brian's Hope'

Love Is A Gamble

Brian:

She will soon be mine. No, it is not the day of "Valentine," but yet and still, she will be mine. She does not know it yet, but she will. I pray that she feels like I feel. She knows that I like her a whole lot. I hope the happiness we share, never stops. When we are together, it is like a different world. I really want her to be my girl.

When we hug, there is a feeling I can not explain. I am the engine and all she has to do is board my train. Her charm is so unique. Her personality is so sweet. She is such a beautiful queen. One day she might wear my ring. Her intelligence is one of a scholar. The conversation is lovely when I call her. She will soon be mine. She is oh so fine. She will soon be mine. The love for me, she shall find. She will soon be mine. She is the reason for this rhyme.

See, I want you but if I don't tell you, you may never know. I mean, I really want you to be the star of my show. I want to be at the front of the church waiting for your hand, not on the back row, mad because my "want to be wife" is marrying another bro. Even if we never marry, I want to be like the kid saying, "with me, will you go"? You know, go with me? Will you be my girlfriend? If I never tell you, you may never know that I want to be with you until the end.

I want to help you stay strong and not break down or bend. Allow me to share my life with you, as we win. We will strive to live right and not put energy into sin. Quit "tripping" girl. Meet my mama "nem." Meet my next of kin. I want you but if I don't tell you, I might miss out. In so many words I told you, but I must need to shout. Lets' build together like a brand new house. I want you but if I don't tell you, you may never be my spouse.

I'm just saying, baby I really want you to be mine, but if it never happens, I guess that will be fine. O. k., I cain't help it. I'm lying, because it will not be fine! I want to have your back like a spine. I want us to be together for an eternal time. Let's stick together like cone and pine. Before any other woman, you are my prime. Pretty woman, you are a "dime". I really want you to be mine, and what I admire most is your mind. If I was a cat; I would want you to be in all my lives, yes, all nine. Let me walk beside you. Please, don't fall behind. Up the tree of prosperity, we will climb. Like the sun, "woman, you shine." Let's have a candle light dinner. Let's wine and dine.

From my heart, I mean every last one of these lines. To love you, I am inclined. It is with you that I want to bind. I, pray that you see it my way and stop being so blind. The things I speak of go way beyond, "R Kelley's "Bump and Grind". Maybe; on the paper, both of our names will be signed. I really want you to be mine. Just say the words and I will not decline. I want to stick with you like "pork and pine." I want to grow with you like, "castle vines". If you say, "no," it will hurt but I will not whine. You have a beautiful personality and "da*n you fine"! Hopefully it will happen in a matter of time. I'm attracted to you like "Lilly" was to "Herman Frankenstein". I want to come together with you like "afros becoming twined". I don't know what it is, but you must be my kind. I just want you to know that, I really want you to be mine.

Nia:

Love, I'm glad you feel that way but I'm not sure if I'm ready today. I'm kind of scared like fast car rides. I like being by your side. Thank you for letting me know but right now, I'm enjoying this vibe. I really like the way we flow. Believe me, I will let you know, and I will take it into serious consideration. Hopefully, I won't take too long and wear out your patience.

Narrator:

A few months have passed by and Brian and Nia were still hitting it off. They were not official, but they were more than friends.

Brian:

Did you change your mind? I often wonder if you've changed your mind. See, there was once upon a time, that I let you know how I felt in a few lines. I told you that I wanted you to be mine. I wanted to have your back like a spine. To get to the top with you, I stay ready to climb.

I love to write about you in my rhymes. Time and time again, I remind you that you are beautiful and fine. You turned me down once, but I will keep trying. I'm gone stay strong, so you won't see this grown man crying. If I told you I loved you, I wouldn't be lying.

You compliment me like "lemon does the lime". It is you that I want to find. On a scale from "1 to 8", you still go past "9". If you say yes, I promise to not leave you behind. I told you that I want you to be my prime. I'm not trying to be "slick". I'm not trying to be "grime". For your love, I am greedy as "swine". If it is against the law to be with you, I don't mind committing that crime. I was just wondering if you had changed your mind?

Nia:

O. k., let me be completely honest. I just don't know yet. I haven't changed my mind, but I still haven't made up my mind. I am still weighing the pros and cons. You are really a great guy. I just don't know if I can keep up with your life style. Maybe we should just take some time apart and get to know ourselves first.

{Scene fades out and comes back up with Brian only}

Brian:

She wants me, but she is scared. For a man like me, she was not prepared. I believe that for me, she truly cares, but to her, I am the type of man that takes too many dares. I am a "hot boy" and for her, that is rare. Soon as she called me, I was there, but she is almost scared to call. She said, "I live life too fast" and reach for things that are too tall. She said she didn't want to get in my way and make me stall. Into the wrong place she doesn't want me to fall. She said, I should learn to dribble before "I ball". All I want to do is get paid like "Bill Gates and Lou Rawls". She is not used to being around so much "live action". She was not ready to be "starting something like "Michael Jackson". I could tell she was scared by her reactions. It is her that I am trying to traction. She was scared to admit it but there was an attraction.

Love Is A Gamble

ACT VI

'The Beautiful and The Bold'

{Tommy sits at his desk in his office and writes his thoughts on paper.}

Tommy:

To my future wife if I ever have one. I am there to help raise my daughters and sons. I will try to help you have so much fun. You may already be in my life and I don't know you are the one. I'm still in the race that I have not yet won. I just wonder what my life will be like when it is all said and done.

I will try to help lift you up when you get down. You and I together will take trips out of town. I will be faithful. There will be no reason to "get around". You will be my adjective, verb, and noun. I truly love life. I am just wondering about my future wife. I want to connect with you like the wind connecting with a kite. With you, I want to reach higher heights.

You will be handled with care like diamonds and pearls. I will be straight up with you. There is no reason to curl. I pray that our marriage becomes a success. I hope we can ignore gossip and mess. To please my extravagant wife, I will not rest. I have many friends but, I hope my wife becomes my best.

I will love you from head to toe. We will help each other grow. This is reality baby. This ain't just no show. I'm getting "turned up" from writing this for some reason. I mean, I don't understand it. I cain't explain it, but we will try to own instead of renting or leasing. I wish I could play my future on film just, so I could be peeking. My love for my wife will be real love, so when I ask to marry you; just say, "I will" before we kiss and hug.

{Tiffany walks in as Tony is writing}

Tiffany:

How you doing, bae? I brought you some lunch. I got your message. What did you want to tell me?

Tommy:

Baby, I was just thinking about you.

Tiffany:

What's on your mind, bae?

Tommy:

I want to love you but don't know how. It can be one million peo-ple and you still stand out in the crowd. I don't know how to love because I don't know if I've ever loved before. My feelings for you, I can not ignore.

You make me feel funny inside. I want to love you and from that, I can no longer hide. I want to love you so could you please assist? When you are not with me, you are truly missed. Waiting on you, I'll mess around and become old and gray, so what I am asking is, "can I love you, today"?

When I thought I was in love, I was only a child. I was infatuated, lustful, and just being wild. I don't understand. I wish I didn't have this feeling. I am falling for you like "twin tower" buildings. I know that if it never happens, I need to move on. I want to love you or am I wrong? I want to love you but don't know how. It could be one million people and you would still stand out in the crowd.

Tiffany:

Just let go and let nature take its course. If it is meant to be, it will be. I don't want you to feel so pressured. You gone mess around and give yourself a heart attack. Love can be easy. Stop trying to make it so hard.

Love Is A Gamble

Tommy:

I'm always thinking about you. Last night, I woke up at four in the morning with you on my mind, so I sat on the porch with "Mary" and started writing this rhyme. For some reason, I can not stop thinking of you. I guess I must not really want to. With all do respect, you are "the sh*t," and I would rather stay together and not split. I can not believe you are running through my mind like you are. You and I together shine like the rims on a foreign car. You and I together make a da*n good team. Am I, really awake or is this a dream? If I am dreaming just let me sleep. It is you that my 3rd and physical eyes peep. I don't know if I'm lost without you, but I am glad that I am found. You have been my life jacket when I was about to drown.

Even when you are not around, I feel so much affection. Maybe you are up at four in the morning and we are making the same mental connection, or maybe you are dreaming about me as you sleep. Maybe I'm wrong and should feel like a geek. Regardless of the situation, it is you that is on my mind. So as "Ms. Jane" and I sit on the porch, it is to you that we dedicate this rhyme.

Tiffany:

I wasn't up and, I wasn't dreaming, but I cain't stop thinking of you. It is time for me to tell you my truth. I thought of the time I had no food to eat. You invited me over for a seat, at your personal kitchen table. I was hungry, so I was willing and able. I thought of the time you told me not to worry, when my best friend was being buried. You told me that my life goes on, and to hold my head up and stay strong. I thought of the time when I was walking down the street. You gave me a ride, so I could take the load off my feet. I thought of all your encouraging words. Everything you said, I heard. I just can't stop thinking of you, and bae, that is the truth.

Tommy:

Thank you for that truth because you always stay on my mind. Sometimes, I consciously try to make you leave my thoughts, but my sub conscious will not let you walk. It keeps telling me that you are the one I need. Deep inside I am trying to believe, but I didn't want to jump to the wrong conclusion. I want to stick around and not go out like fusion.

You stay on my mind constantly. I cain't wait until my thoughts become my reality. In my mind, you are on display like crockery. You are planted inside of me like pottery. It is a must that I have you. It is sobriety. For you to be a part of my life is a necessity. Don't break my heart because I'm not always subtlety. You are more than a picture. You are crafty. You are the one for me undisputedly. With you, I am free. Without you, I am back in slavery.

I pray that we; one day, become "we". I cain't hide it anymore. I admit that I am guilty. You stay on my mind all night and daily. With you, I want to spend an eternity. Seriously, with you, it should be infinity. I feel you when you are not here like ghostly. For you, I have to keep my ethics together like morality, and these words can be considered embroidery. It is you that I want especially. It is you that I want particularly. Woman, you are so notably. I give you praise while you live like a, eulogy. Without you, I am a bad note. With you, I am harmony. You are the woman I love to see. You are always, on my mind.

Love Is A Gamble

ACT VII

'In Another World'

Love Is A Gamble

{Gary goes to the library and e-mails his lady}

Gary:

To the one I love: From the one who loves you: I have known you for some time now. We have taught each other how, to love and respect woman and man. The love for you is a love that others can not understand. You were there when no one else was around. Your presence lifted me up when I was down. Your smile would bring sunshine to my surroundings. Your hand pulled me up when I was drowning.

When you hold me, there is a feeling I can not explain. You have been there to comfort me in my deepest pain. Just to hear your voice is pleasing to my ear. You have helped me overcome some of my fears.

Sometimes, I sit and think of the good times we've had. Thank you for the comfort when I was sad. You have been one that I could tell all my troubles to; however, I kept most of them to myself knowing they would worry you. To me, you have been such a big inspiration. You've helped me to become a much better person. You helped me solve my problems when I was not for certain. If I don't say anything else, I just want to say, "I thank you" and remember that my love for you will always be true.

Narrator:

He wants to go to the next level. He does not claim to be an "angel or a horny devil". She started something that he wants to help finish. He knows he will be good for her like spinach. Since she took the chance to flirt, he has to try to help make something work. When he first saw her, she caught his eye. The next level is what he wants to try.

She smiles and looks him in the face when they speak. If she was a game of chess he would not cheat, because he wants every move to be the right move. He wants to massage her skin that is smooth. He tells her exactly what is on his mind. It goes way beyond these poetic lines. He is not sure what the next level will be. He just wants to experiment and see.

Gary:

Woman, what have you done to me? I don't know if I am dreaming or if it is reality. I might be a fool for letting you know these feelings inside of me. My feelings for you are starting to go on a spree, and I promise that I want them to slow down. I'm glad that you and I were found. You are a queen and I want you to wear my crown. My love for you adds up by the pound. You saw the man in me when everyone else saw a clown. My thoughts and feelings are spinning like a merry-go-round. I am trying to stop the spin before I get sick. Please, let me know if my feelings should quit, because I know I am jumping the gun and sh*t. It is you that I truly want to be with.

I really cain't believe that I am writing this rhyme. If you were a mountain, I would love to climb. I want to move forward with you and not look behind. It is to you that I want to give my time. You know by now that I will keep trying. My feelings, I am no longer denying. Woman, what have you done to me?

Because, I seem to be stuck on you. I'm stuck on you like "super glue". With you I never feel "blue". I know you have realized this. I have given you several clues. I "dig you baby" and this is the news. I want to be a pair like "Jordan" tennis shoes. You are the woman that I choose. Lovely lady, I want to take you on a cruise. Your heart, I will never try to bruise. When they ask, "who is your husband", I want to be accused. Your love, I will never abuse. You blow my mind like a fuse. You are sweet to me like the candy "JuJu's". With you on my team, it will be hard to lose. Let's go see the world. Lets' make some moves. When I'm with you, I stay in a good mood.

I will tell the world. I will not be mute. You make me feel good like "ooze". I admire that you stay on your p's and q's. If marriage has directions, I will follow the rules. Just thinking of you, makes my mind soothe. You take the bumps out of my road to make it smooth. Let's work

Love Is A Gamble

it out like a carpenter's tool, and I pray you feel the same way too. You make me nervous. Yes, you do. All I know is that, "I'm stuck on you."

ACT VIII

'Guiding Right'

Michael:

I appreciate the way you make me feel, and believe me, this is on the real. God has dealt me a good deal. When you come around, I get a thrill. You help take my pain away like a "hydro codeine pill." On me, I appreciate the love that spills. I appreciate the pretty smiles from your face. I value every second with you. Time does not waste. I needed you on my team like a "Perry Mason" case. I am learning to not rush and just keep a steady pace. Like shoe strings, I am ready to tie up the lace. I want our love to last long like a marathon race. Be honest with me. Don't make me chase. If needed, I will give you space. I am thankful for being in this place. I don't think you realize that you are sweet like "sugar inside of cake".

I hope we stay together for a long time. I really mean every, last one of these lines. You make me feel good. I feel just fine. I hope you are listening with an open mind. You inspire me to keep pushing forward and not fall behind. I just want to say that I appreciate the way you make me feel one more time.

Carmen:

I appreciate you too, honey. I don't know how to put it in words like you be doing but I really appreciate you too. I feel so relaxed around you. I used to be so uptight. I was almost ready to leave you men alone. It seemed like no one treated me right. No one would be a real man. They were just boys; and then, you came along. Thank you for just being you and so good to me.

Michael:

If I could have a conversation with your mother or father, I would let them know how much I love their daughter. I would ask for their opinion about our relationship. I would tell them that I am there for you in health and sick. I would let them know that I would do anything for you, and I would remind them that my words are true. I would tell them that it would be up to you if you wanted to work. I just thank God for adding you to the Earth.

I would work to provide you with the finer things. You would be the queen and I would be the king. I would let them know that you will be treated with respect. I wouldn't mind working just to let you rest. I would tell them that, "God" would be in our lives. I would want only a wife and not wives. I love you with all my heart and soul. With you, I hope to grow old. If I had a conversation with your mother or father, I would let them know how much I love their daughter.

Carmen:

They know you love me. We talk about you all the time.

Michael:

What yall be saying?

Carmen:

Don't worry about that. Just know that, they know that you truly love me. They really like you and that is not normal for my dad. He told me that you have potential and that everything is going to be all right. Well; honey, I'm going home. I have to get up early for work in the morning. I love you. I'll call you when I get home.

{About a hour and a half goes by and Michael sends Carmen a message through the "d.m."}

Michael:

I just figured out that you couldn't call if you wanted to. I got worried, so I tried to call you, to see if you made it home, but my communication system was not on. The reason it is off is because I didn't pay the bill to my telephone. Like a science experiment, I wish you were cloned, so I could still be with you and not be alone. I love it when you are here. I hate it when you are gone. I hope we one day share a home. I really "cut for you" and this is already known.

I felt like; because I didn't call you, I was wrong, so I sent subliminal messages through my dome. I prayed that you made it back to where you reside. I hated to hear you tell me bye. When you walked through the door, I noticed you from the corner of my eye. I want you to forever be on my side. I talk to my friends about you like it was the "knot that we already tied". I know I need to slow down and stop trying to fly. I need to be cool and just glide.

I want to come along for more than just the ride. Every time I see you, I light up like it was a surprise. Maybe I'm trying too hard even though it feels like I haven't tried. I know I might be getting off the subject, but I cain't help it. I love it. I want to connect with you like corny dogs and mustard. With you, I'm w-d 40. Without you, I am rusted. You need to stop playing and become "Mrs. Munson." You need to gone and be wifey, so I can be your husband, but anyway you didn't ask me all that but that's why I'm messaging you, because I know you couldn't call.

{Carmen messages him back}

Carmen:

Yes, I did try to call and, I did make it home. Thank you for checking on me but you have to do better honey. You always forget to pay your bill on time. That is not good but anyway, when will it be back on.

Michael:

First thing in the morning.

Carmen:

> Ok, good night. Love you

Michael:

> Love you too...

Love Is A Gamble

ACT IX

'All These Days In Our Lives'

George:

I'm not sorry. I know it sounds harsh but if I keep saying I'm sorry, "I'll become sorry." Baby, we old school like "Sega and Atari". I am not sorry like "Ruben Studdard". I am not sorry for being a strong brother.

Baby, I wish you could see the picture that you can't seem to see. Baby, I promise that I don't try to make you grieve, and I know there are some things that I need to work on. Yes, I admit that at times, I am wrong. I know that is hard to believe but it is true. Baby, just know that I really love you. I'm not sorry for strongly looking out for our future, and baby when we get married, I'm going to be "wearing you out like Kamasutra".

Veronica:

You are soooo dang gone stubborn. Saying you are sorry doesn't make you sorry. Are you sure you are ready for the next level? Its not just going to be you when we take this step. It is going to be us, and can you think about more than just sex all the time, please?

George:

I know baby. I'm working on the new me. I'm trying to get better. Lets just enjoy this day. Lets' enjoy this moment. After all, it is "Valentines Day". Speaking of that, I wrote you something. Check it out.

Pretty lady, "Happy Valentines Day". For a woman like you, I get on my knees and pray. On me is where I want your love to spray. Into the perfect couple, I want us to mold together like clay. Into me, your love should intercalate. I hope we stay together and not separate. To see you again, I can not wait. You help make my crooked paths, straight. To make this relationship better, I will not procrastinate. I am speaking the truth. I am not trying to dissimulate.

With you by my side, I feel so much affection. I knew when our paths crossed, I had taken the right direction. I caught these feelings like an interception. I know I am not perfect but with you, I am close to perfection. I mean this. I make no corrections. In your life, I am glad to have a section. My love for you, I don't question. You keep me standing strong like an erection. Pretty lady, "Happy Valentines Day" and thank you for being such a blessing.

Veronica:

Thank you honey. That was so sweet. Now I have something for you. First; of all, I know you work a lot, so I just wanted you to relax. As you are taking your shower, I will be getting ready for you to "break my back." When you are done, all you have to do is lay on the bed and I will rub you down with lotion and give you the best massage you ever had. Then, after we "make love", I have reservations for us at a place I know you will love.

{They are in the restaurant sitting at the table. George has a big surprise. He pulls a ring out.}

George:

Without love, there is no life. So, baby, will you please be my wife. Can we walk hand and hand into eternity, and one day I pray that you have our baby. You are the one I choose, and I am the one you chose. Forever with you is how I want to grow. You are my everything and so much more. I am ready to carry you through the door. We are not "slaves" so we don't have to "jump the broom". I'm ready for you to be my bride and I'm ready to be your groom. My "life jacket" is what you are. You help give me drive like "NASSCAR". I won't let you down. Just believe. You are exactly what I need. I want to provide you with all your needs and wants. Together, we gone make music like, "Avant". Without love, there is no life, so baby, "will you please be my wife"?

Veronica:

Yes! Yes! Yes! I will! Of course, I will be your wife!

{They kiss and hug. The other patrons in the restaurant applaud.}

George:

I will be your husband and you will be my wife. Together, we will live this life. Between us, there will be no strife. We will love each other just alike. I am the wheels and you are the bike. With you, I want to reach higher heights. Our marriage is not wrong. It is only right. You are my princess and I am your knight. Together, we shine bright. You are the electricity and I am the light.

I hope it is not true that couples fight. If we do, I hope everything will be alright. I have to have you by any means. We are a beautiful couple, I deem. I will help try to bring life to your greatest dreams. I can't wait for our marriage scene. You flow through me like a stream. You have lifted me like a space ships "beam". My shoulder is here if you need to lean. I think I am really going to like this marriage thing. I love you with all my heart, soul, body, and mind. I thank God that I am all yours and that you are all mine.

ACT X

'As The World Turns and Turns Again'

{Scene takes place at the reception, after the wedding. Jeremy is on stage.}

Jeremy:

Well, I's married now. It is just the first day, but I will learn how. If anyone opposes, the exit is that way. No matter what, "this woman is my wife, today". She is my wife today and forever more. Like I said, "If you oppose, you can walk out the door. As a matter of fact, you need to run before you get whooped. Off, of us, all haters will be "shook." I married the one that loved me and now I'm hooked. You can now find us together in the "county books".

She is my people. She is not a stranger. I have known her ever since we were fifth graders. Let it be known that this is "wifey". This is my woman. I would not give her up for nothing. We look good. Don't you agree? I thank God for sending this woman to me. What you ask for, you truly get. I promise that I will never quit. We got what we were looking for. We are legit. You keep me "hard like Acme Bricks". I cain't wait for you to "ride me like "Mitts".

I want to thank my "in-laws" for having a girl and not a dude. For that, "I truly thank you". This is the woman I truly adore and love. We fit together like hand in glove. We fit like foot and sock. We fit like dirt and rock. We fit like water and fish. We fit like "Geni" and wish. We are perfect together, ya dig, and if you disagree, you can keep your comments.

For this woman, I am truly "down". In my life, a true friend is what I found. Now I have me a help mate. She gives me reason to cele-brate. I am hers like she is mine. Together, we will grind. Together we will shine. With her, I am in front. Without her, I'm behind. With her, I want to party like, "Prince" in 1999." To all you "cats" that told me, "marriage doesn't work out," I ain't got the same woman you had or got so rest your mouth. Just because yours was bad, don't mean that for me though. I'm a grown man. I knew what I was doing when I proposed.

Narrator:

Half a year has gone by and the reality sets in. No one is there but the married couple. The priest is gone. The wedding party is not around. All the family and friends are gone too. The wedding ceremony was just that. It was a ceremony. That is the early part. The real deal is the fact that you have to live this thing called marriage. Sometimes your spouse might need a little reassurance to know that everything is going to be o.k. They need to know that when you get married, that is exactly what you intend to do and that is, "be married".

{Time goes on and they just made it to see their first wedding anniversary.}

Jeremy:

Baby, "Happy Anniversary". For you, I stay thirsty. For you, I stay hungry. I thank God that we are not lonely. I am so grateful that you crossed my path. We must be o.k. because these twelve months have gone by fast. I cain't believe, I actually married my best friend. I got tired of doing the same ole thing again and again. I also appreciate that you look good, and I pray that we stick together like nail in wood.

I thank God for this occasion. I can't wait for the second year to be in this situation. You "push me" and give me so much motivation. I have access to satellite and cable but I'm not changing stations. I'm staying tuned in like a radio. As long as I live, it is with you that I want to grow. No matter how many performers there are, you are always the "star" of my show.

You are there when its easy and when its hard. Like I said, "you are my super star. "Foxy mama", you need to be in a movie. "I can dig you baby. You are groovy." Its been a year but we are not new to the scene, and please don't wake me if this is a dream, because I am really enjoying myself. I know you are right so there is no reason to "go left." I need a real woman by my side, and we have a full tank baby, so lets' ride. We have a whole bunch of life to live. We have so much to receive and so much to give.

As long as you are on my side, we will rise to the top, and we will not stop. There is always more to it than meets the eye. I still remember the first time you came by, and I look forward to the next moment I see your beautiful face. Happy anniversary and I love you every day.

Narrator:

One thing that never ends is time. Time goes on forever. Over time, married couples still are trying to learn, each other. Emotions get involved. Some start to question marriage.

Shante':

Baby, I was watching this movie last night. It was about this married couple. The man was cheating on his wife and she kept giving him extra chances. I know it was just a movie, but it got me to thinking. Is there anything going on with you that I need to know about?

Jeremy:

Don't worry, you are the one. Outside of you, there is none. You are the only one that "gets some". I hate to see you leave but I love to see you cum. Oh, I'm sorry. I may have spelled that wrong. Our relationship is like a beautiful love song. We are not children anymore. We are grown. I am the king and you are the queen of this throne. My love for you is a grant. It is not a loan. I have a wife now so there is no reason to roam. Without you, I rent. With you, I own. Marrying you is not wrong, and on another note, "I love to bone". I have never loved a woman like I love you and let that be known.

We are a team baby like, "Cheech and Chong". We are a team baby like, "Pippin and Jordone". We are a team baby like, "government and clones". I need your support. You help make me strong. I want to stick with you like a cactus in Arizone. Without you, I kick field goals. With you I make it into the end zone. We shine like chrome. Don't worry, you are the one. Other than you, there is none.

Shante':

Thank you for assuring me that there is nothing to worry about. I am truly committed to you. I know I have been stressed out and worried lately. I am so sorry, baby. I'm just scared. I don't want to, loose you. Just bare, with me. I am trying to get better. I love you so much...

Jeremy:

I love you too, baby....

Narrator:

The married couple is hanging in there. They have made it passed the first few years of marriage. It hasn't been easy every day, but they are learning how to work together. It is anniversary time again.

Jeremy:

Happy anniversary. I know it has been rough lately. I love you with all my heart and soul. I pray to God that you and I together grow old. Never give up on me and I promise to do the same. I'm so glad that you took my last name. These years with you have been the best years of my life. Thank you for being my wife.

I know I am not the perfect husband but thank you for all your loving. Thank you for the time we share. Baby, I will always be there; there meaning, here. I pray for us to see many more years. This is our special day. I would not trade it, no way. You help make me strong. Marrying you was not wrong. Happy anniversary baby. It is going to get better than how it has been lately.

ACT XI

'Hard Knocks Landing'

Joe:

I don't know if I deserve you. Without you, I don't know what I would do. You are my beautiful wife. You are the one I think about day time and night. It may not always seem like it but in you, I delight. Everyday of my life; not seeing you, is a fight. Inside of me, I be throwing "upper cuts, elbows, lefts, and rights."

I just want us to go the distance like a 10k race. Together, we are always in first place. Stay down with me baby and I promise you that we will come up. You have to love me even when I seem to be stuck. When I am stuck, I will still stay in drive. I love to have you by my side. It won't be this rough for long. We will be alright if we just hold on. We need to hold on to our faith in God. I don't mean to hurt you. That's not what I'm about. It hurts me to see you hurt like you do. It might not seem like it at times, but I always love you.

Carla:

I know you don't mean to hurt me, but you do. You think it is still just all about you. You act like you are not even married. You are just still doing what you want to do. You don't give your family no kind of consideration. I am trying to be patient but its hard. Baby, its hard...

{Joe walks away and goes to his room where he starts to think to himself.}

The voice in the head of Joe:

I don't think my wife likes me anymore. To her, I have become such a bore. This is not the first time she didn't like me though. Back in the day, she told me I can get my sh*t and go. See, I don't think it is as bad as it was back then. This time, she hasn't brought up divorce. She hasn't said that she wants it to end. Back then, she actually hated me, and times were tough for us financially.

I've been feeling this pain in my gut, and I tried to talk to her about it instead of letting it build up. Letting it build up will make me explode. I wish I knew what I don't know. I know I might be jumping the gun. I just might be. I know that if I look for trouble, it will find me, so I'm closing my eyes and praying that it just passes me by. I can't let her see me cry.

She wants time to herself. I asked if I could do anything to help. We used to go out together. She's going out on her own and seems to dress even sexier. She wants to be alone. My house doesn't feel like a home. She always runs across town. I keep checking the mirror to see if I look like a clown. I know I'm in my emotions, but I've been married to this woman for several years, and I just don't want to look like "Willie Fu Fu" after I finish these tears.

I'm married but feel so separated. I don't like it. I really hate it. I'm trying to pull myself together the best way that I can. I wonder if it is another woman or another man. I wonder if it is nobody at all. It might not even be nothing when she gets those phone calls. I just wonder who it is when it silently rings. I might be "tripping" off of all these things. I guess time will tell as it always does. I wish broken hearts were not a part of love, but they seem to be, because I don't think my wife likes me.

Narrator:

They are married but they may as well be roommates. He still remembers their first date. I'm not saying she doesn't remember but I only talked to him. The information I have didn't come from them. He said they were just married on paper. He thought marriage would be so much greater. He thought it was going to be like on t.v. He thought it was going to be like "The Obamas and The Cosby's". He said that they may as well get twin beds, because he doesn't get in between her legs. He said they used to go out all the time. Now, she seems so hard to find. He goes out alone, because she is always gone.

He just once again wants to be involved. What does it take to get this problem solved? He is just trying to ignore the situation, because she gets real defensive when he tries to have the conversation. He asked her was anything going on. He asked why she needs to leave the room to talk on the phone. He asked who she was going out with. He asked who keeps giving her all the gifts. She said she was tired of all the questions, so she leaves him just guessing. His gut keeps telling him that something is not right. The roommate doesn't trust his wife.

They used to have so much fun. Now, they seem to be done. Marriage is not sweet like it used to be. For better or worse is starting to look a little bleak. He is so confused and don't know what to do. One spouse will lie just to live the other spouse's truth. They've been together for some time now. He wonders if he should have left the first time she told him to get out. He wonders if it is wrong. He wonders if she will just walk away. We'll wait and see. Until then, he is really trying to love his roommate.

The problem is, she has been looking for her daddy. That's the man that always made her happy. That's the man that always put food on the table. He is the man that told her to watch out for "Caine and Able". She is a preachers' kid. She had to be sneaky with some of the things that she did, because them "church folks" be watching. They cain't wait to tell "Rev. Slawson". "Pastor, I don't mean to be messy, but I saw your daughter..." Now she is grown and still looking for her father, but she searches for him in different men. No one seemed to match up to him.

See, now he's past away. He went on to a better place. She never planned for him to leave that soon. She had the closest thing to her dad with her first groom, but he still just wasn't daddy. He didn't quite make her happy. They had been married some time and eventually divorced. They were on an opposite course. A new guy sweet talks her and makes his move. She is venerable and doesn't recognize that she is being used. People try to tell her, but she doesn't listen. She can not find a man to qualify for that position.

She was introduced to a new world. She felt young again; not like a little girl but you know like in her twenties. Trying to find the one, she was willing to go through plenty. She was ready to move around again. Once again, she was looking for a new man, that could remind her of her pops. She was determined. She would not stop.

She needed to introduce herself to "herself," and leave them men on the shelf. See, she's never been without a man, so to be alone, she doesn't understand, and daddy is gone. Baby girl has to realize that she is grown. Baby girl needs to move right along, and enjoy herself before she calls the next wrong person on that phone.

Love Is A Gamble

ACT XII

'My True Passion'

Tyrone:

To my spectacular and beautiful wife: I love you day time and night. Being with you is not wrong. It has to be right. With you on my team, we reach higher heights, and forever with you is how I want to live my life. You make my insides float like a kite. For your love, I will continue to fight. In the darkness, you help provide light. You make all of my days so bright. Woman, I love you and you are such a delight. Even when you are not here, I have you in sight. Talking about you, I could forever write. You are the lady that I love and that I like. I love when you ride me like a bike. For you, I would take a chance with my life. When I am with you, I feel no strife.

You have been such an inspiration. Without you, I am Texas. With you, I become a whole nation. You bring me so much motivation. I am only the track and you are the train station. You run through me like liquidation. With you, there is no irritation. I would rather be early than to have you waiting. I would rather love you than to be hating. You are the woman I love and there is no debating. On a scale from 1 to 10, you get the highest rating. I dedicate this to my spectacular and beautiful wife. I love you every day and I love you every night.

Amy:

Falling in love with you has been a dream come true. I looked forward to this all my life. I had a great example. My parents were married for many years. Today is a new day and I am glad to share it with you. You will always have a special place in my heart. When I look at you or think about you, I feel like the luckiest lady in the world. I am now and forever here for you. For the rest of my life, I pray that we stay together as husband and wife. With every ounce of me, I am loving you. I love you so much...

Tyrone:

I love you too. You are my beautiful queen. When I see you, it makes a better scene, and when you depart the scene, I begin to wish it was a dream. To me, you are my everything. You are the stars in the sky. You are the answer to the question "why". You are my sun shine. You are so divine.

You are my beautiful queen. You are a diamond like in your wedding ring. You comfort me like a beautiful song that one might sing. You are the other half of this king. You are lovely like the weather in spring. You are my beautiful queen.

Your ancestors are the mothers of the Earth, and I thank you for giving my children birth. More than riches and gold, you are worth. Beautiful, I thank you and I promise to help make this work. I will help you however I can. With a strong woman by your side, you have to be a strong man. I am your number one fan, and I love being a part of your brand.

We just celebrated another anniversary. I remember the day we hooked up. It was on a Thursday. I thought I was slick like butter. I was a bachelor. I didn't know how to be a lover, but I sure am learning with time. A marriage takes the body, spirit, and mind, to make it all really work. Most of the time it is good but at other times, it hurts. To be married this many years took blood, sweat, and tears but it has also been healing, love, and good times. She is the only one for me. I thank God that she is mine. If I had to start all over, I would do it again. Without her, I loose. With her, I win. Can we try our best to have harmony? I won't lie. It hasn't always been "holy matrimony". That is just what they say at the ceremony, and thanks and no thanks to all the people for advice. I know you all meant well, but that was my wife under that veil. I look forward to the future looking better for us two. Woman, I really love you. I thought it was all about me but I now understand that God runs my reality. I pray that we have many more anniversaries to come. I thank God for sending me the right one.

Amy:

I thank God that I am your wife. You help complete my life. Thank you for all that you have done. We came together like two halves that make one. We make a good fit like "Ruby Huxtable and Budd". Thank you for all your love. Thank you for raising our children with me. I love you and I am exactly where I want to be.

I hope we stay together like it will never be over. You have the key that starts my motor. I love you more than I can express. I think we are perfect together. We are the best. No matter what the world has to say, I love you every night and I love you every day. I really am glad that I am your wife. I thank God for you being a part of my life.

ACT XIII

'Too Hot For TV,
But Not Too Hot For Me"

Love Is A Gamble

Stephon:

(Sing 1st line) Ain't no woman like the one I got. She makes me feel high like "one that might inhale "medicinal pot". You get it? She makes me feel good. If I had to start over with her, I would. I would do it three or four times and again. I met her when I was 9 or 10. I was a boy and she was a girl. It was back in the day and she still had a curl, but now its years later and some months, ya dig. She has blessed me with beautiful kids. She truly is the love of my life. I thank God for my wife.

She is my best friend. I plan on being with her until the end. She helps complete me like the last puzzle piece. We make a good fit like vagina and peneice. Speaking of that, I shole hope I get me some. I have to make sure I don't get too drunk, because I be at the club "talking all that jazz." Then I get to the house and fall asleep real fast, but that ain't happening tonight! She gone have to ride this "bike", and she can sit anywhere she d*mn, please. Sometimes, she likes for me to freeze, just so she can work the "hula hoop" in her hips. I be like, "got da*n, what the ph*ck, ooooh sh*t, but anyway, (sing) ain't no woman like the one I got. She makes me feel high like "one that might inhale "medicinal pot." You get it? She makes me feel good. If I had to start over with her, I would.

{Sophia just finished freshening up. She walks in the room and Stephon starts to say...}

Stephon:

Baby, I really like the way you over there looking. You are "hot" like the kitchen where the chef be cooking. You are "hot" like "California" wild fire. You are "hot" like the sun that sits up higher. You have the most "dreamy" eyes. I love your lips; even the ones between your thighs. I am serious so don't laugh. All I want to do is "act bad". Hold me so very close. Think of me as the most. My hands are rubbing up and down your thighs. I love how wet it is inside. Your legs are in the air as your calves, rest on my shoulders. I'm ready to give you this "dill" like its "Kosher".

Put one leg over there. Leave the other one over here. Feel me as I cum through your house. Let me know if you want to be "choked out". Every time I "hit it", I want to "hit it" better than the last time. You are the true definition of "fine". Lock your legs like a knot. I'm going to give you this magic stick until you tell me to stop". Da*n them clocks! I'm not worried about the time. I'm just glad that you are all mine.

I'm trying to make you feel like never before. Its o.k. to be greedy because I have so much more. New positions, we will create. This is the real deal. This is not fake. Woman, let's act bad! I promise to give it all I got. I just hope you give it all you have.

Sophia:

I like it when you give it to me like that. I like it when you hit it from the back, and what do you mean, let you know if I want to be choked? I don't know about that. I don't know if I want your hands wrapped around my throat, but I love when you give me that "daddy long stoke". I don't like it rough all the time, but sometimes I like being hand cuffed like I committed crime. I love for you to pound it like cake. I love to put this cookie all in your face, and I love the way you taste. You make me cum across the finish line like I broke the tape. With you, all I do is win, and I truly love my man. I cain't wait for you to "hit it" again. I love to cum and I hate for it to end.

Stephon:

At least that gives us something to look forward to. I thank God every time I penetrate you. I cain't wait to get freaky again tonight. I cain't wait for my "3rd leg" to reach its highest height. Soon as you get home and park the car, you won't have to go very far, because I will carry you so won't have to walk. Every time I think of you, I get hard like sidewalk chalk.

I will bring you in and lay you on the bed. I will massage you from toe to head. I will massage every, body part. I cain't wait to stick you like darts. After your massage, I will carry you to the shower. Your beauty blossoms like a flower. I will wash your back and turn so you can wash mine. You will tingle up and down your spine. After we have washed our bodies clean, we can finish some of the fantasies that we see in our dreams.

It is your body that I love to taste. I will give you my full potential. Not an ounce will waste. I am here to fulfill your every need. I want to plant in you, my seed. You are my exotic plant. I will never forget the first time I saw you dance. You had me "phening" for more. Every time you dropped it, I wished I was the floor, but that is another story. Without "Viagra", you still keep me "horny". I know I've talked enough sh*t. I'm just ready to "get that cookie," because I stay ready "to hit".

Sophia:

I'm ready for you to hit it too but I also like it when you take it slow. I love your foreplay. Sometimes, I want it to last forever. When you take it slow with me, you give me time to think. It is almost like you are making love to my mind too. I love you baby and I am ready, but can we start off with a massage?

Stephon:

Are you sure you want a massage today, because before I finish you will be cumming so don't play? I will take every drop of your clothes off. I will massage your body that is so soft. Baby, I will start with your back side. My massage will be exotic like the valley between your thighs. I will massage each toe one by one. Make yourself comfortable. Lets just have fun. I am now rubbing the bottom of your feet. I promise that you will enjoy this massage from me. I have now moved up to your ankles and calves. It may tickle so you might laugh.

You will feel good all through your pores. I guarantee you that you will want more and more. Before I put lotion on your hamstrings, I will give them a kiss. This is a beautiful part that I can't miss. I will massage them with nice and firm strokes. When I get through, you will feel like a feather that floats. My hands have finally reached the hills. On your butt I will let the lotion spill. I'll rub it in on both sides. The "cookie" wants me to put it in from the back and let it hide, but I'm going to hold on and just let it go, because there are so many other things I would like to show. Your back, I rub and massage with a light chop. I promise you will never want my massage to stop. I have just licked your back down the middle. Your part is really, quite simple.

All you have to do is relax. The story I tell you is a fact. Now I am at your neck and your shoulders. My massage will make you feel a lot younger than older. Your neck and shoulders, I kiss too. This body massage is dedicated to you. Now it is time to run my fingers through your hair. I massage your scalp which may seem rare. Now lay on your back queen of queens. My massage will make you have wet dreams. Once again, I am at the left and right foot. Then, at the shins and knees, I take a look. First, I kiss your shins up and down. Without me even looking, I know you have a smile and no frown. Now there goes those thighs, that do not catch me by surprise. I lick them from the outside to the inside. This massage, you can not pass by. On those thighs, I use all ten knuckles. Now it is time for the place close to your belt buckle.

I will handle this precious and sensitive spot with T. L. C. because not only does it mean a lot to you, but it means so much to me. I touched the lips very gentle. For you to be still, I know it is not simple but try to be still as can be. It is you that I want to please. I open the lips and rub the inside. I am letting you know so you won't be so surprised. Now, I am your stomach and chest. Your body is the best. Each breast I gently hold. You are "hot" and no longer cold. I kiss and suck each nipple and remember, your part is really quite simple. All you have to do is relax. Your stomach has also felt my tongue. With this massage, I will have you "sprung." I am now at the front of your shoulders and neck. I hope I qualify on this mas-sage test. I try my best to give it my all. You keep me rising and standing tall.

Sophia:

I almost just came thinking about it. I could almost feel you touching me just by listening to your sexy a*s. I can not wait for my massage. I wish I could get it right now. Now you got me phening like "Jodeci." I know it is just a massage, but it feels like making love. Now I want you to make love to the rest of me.

Stephon:

Just tell me the place and time, because you know sex is always on my mind. You make me hot like your name is "heat." I don't want to stay shallow. I want to go deep. I just want my motion to wave into your ocean. Tell me where you want me to put this "baby lotion." We can do it anywhere from home to a resort. We can have sex like it is a sport.

I will explore all of your body parts. Before we can finish, we first have to start. I will kiss you from head to toe, that's from top to down low. I'm trying to give you all this d-love. I cain't wait for that beautiful valley to cover me like the floor under the rug. I will touch you in places you love to be touched. You will be my dinner, breakfast, and lunch. I want to taste all, of your berries. I want my stem to connect with your cherry. Sex is on my mind for a fact so let me hit it sideways, vertical, front, and back.

{Sophia leans over and whispers in Stephon's ear}

Sophia:

I've been trying to fight this feeling, but I can't help myself. I am ready to give it all to you daddy. I want you to have your way with me. Do with me whatever you, please...

Stephon:

She whispered in my ear. The things she told me, I wanted to hear. I was a man about mine. There was no fear. She wanted me to "hit it" from the rear. She wanted me to "hit it" from the "front and the side." Then she wanted me to lay down, so she could ride. In and out is how she wanted me to slide. She asked if I wanted to "hit it" so I couldn't hide.

I had to step up to the plate. I was hungry for her like I had never ate, and for me to get some "mind" I couldn't wait. I just wanted to feel in her empty space. I felt like a kid waiting to go to the park. I felt like the electricity from an electric spark. I love to hear the "kitty kat" fart. It felt like monopoly every time you pass start, and I was waiting to win the race. I'm ready so I have to tie up the lace. I was trying to cross the finish line in 1st place. We both had that "sex face." I know she came. I didn't have to ask. I was holding her shoulder as I slapped that a*s. I hit it slow and I hit it fast. She came first. I came second and we both came last.

But, sometimes, I really just want to make sweet passionate love. I want to make you feel high as a flying dove. I want to lick every, body part. I am ready for this love making to start. We shall use many different props. I want to make love so long that it feels like we will never stop. The melted chocolate, I will pour. As I use my tongue, you will want more and more. I will feed you exotic berries. I will do just about anything. Just dare me. Would my tongue catch you by surprise, if I start licking you in between those beautiful thighs? I will put you in just the right place. I value every moment so time, I will not waste.

I just want to give you all of my attention. Into your "tunnel of love" enters my extension. Each breast shall be held and kissed. After it is all over, I promise I will be missed. I will give you "love marks" if you wish. They shall come kiss by kiss. Different positions, we will try. I just want to make you feel high like wings that fly. Around us are candles and flowers. After it is over, we will take a shower. With you, I want to make sweet passionate love. I promise to make you feel high like flying doves.

Sophia:

I want you to make love to me like never, before. I love you so much. When you make love to me, I feel like pottery in your hands. You mold me into the perfect piece of art. I love how your brush paints the inside of my walls. You are my "Picasso" but sometimes, "I cain't even lie. I want that "go hard or go home" graffiti artist in you.

Stephon:

I was trying to be gentle but, I see you would rather me "tear it up." I love "ph*cking" just like I love "making love." Either way, I'm still trying to take you to a level above. The whole mood will be just right. Are you ready to board this sexual flight? We can play "r and b or trap music" in the background. My lips are ready for your lips. Are you down? We will finish on the wall what we start in the bed. Before I get it, I mentally see you "getting me ahead."

You've blind folded me and I'm a little scary. I like it bald, but I'm also cool with it being hairy. You can ride me like a carousel, after I lick you from head to heels. I will kiss "her" like it was a mistletoe hanging over that "little door." We made love, but you still wanted more. You told me to "hit it harder, daddy." I was "hitting it" from the back and you said, "slap me." You told me to "make you scream. Make me say your name. Give it to me, daddy". You wanted some pain, so I started hitting it like a hammer hits a nail. Now, I have both hands slapping tail. Call me postal because I'm putting it in the box like mail. You want me to "hit it" like I just got out of jail. Then in one motion, you turned over and your legs made the letter "V". It really looked like your vagina had wings. I turned that "V" into a straight line. I "hit it" like I was reaching for the back of your spine. You told me, "its yours' daddy" so I had to get mine. After this moment, I can't wait till the next time. Are you sure you are ready for me to "tear it up" because like a rabbit, I love to bump."

Narrator:

The moral of this episode is that he loves him some "cookie". He loves it more than, "Ricky loved Lucy". I mean, he really loves him some vagina. He gets face to face with her for a reminder. He loves what is under that skirt. "Cookie" be giving birth. That flower really makes his stem grow. He likes it down there. He likes it down low. He said,

Stephon:

Them "side ways lips" just be looking at me. They be whispering, "come get this cookie". That "oven" be so warm. It feels like a sweater sleeve on my 3rd arm. Sometimes, I just be still and she lets that "cookie" go to work. It heals me like I was hurt. It makes me feel better even when I already feel good. It makes me rock hard like petrified wood. I be wanting to "knock it out" like a boxing match. I like my cookie made from scratch.

With this cookie, I am going to take my time. The "d" ain't going nowhere because you say the "p" is all mine. You make me feel like I created the whole thing. When I'm away from it, I often have dreams. For personal use, I dream that I can just keep it in my pocket. I dream about my screw going into your socket. I dream about swimming in it under water, and my mouth be wide open when I go under. I be like….(smacking lips) I cain't breathe, but I don't mind drowning in it because "cookie" is all I need!

All I know is that "I love me some cookie"! That cookie is so "guchie." I love it like "Cupid" loves being white. I love it like impatient people love green lights. I probably love it so much because that is where I'm from. I love it because it gives life like the sun. I love it like it is the last thing on Earth. We all have, to admit that we all truly loved "cookie" first. That was the first door we went in and out of. Dear "Cookie", I just wanted to express my love.

Sophia:

Da*n. You know what? You are crazy. You crae crae. Come on over here and get this cookie though with yo crazy a*s...

YA DIG...

Paul "Phroze" Munson

Thank you for your support

Love Is A Gamble

About the Author

Paul Munson also known as "Phroze" (pronounced Froze), was born in 1976. He has always been a class act in more ways than one. Paul witnessed poetry being recited at an early age by his mother. This is his second professional book he has created. The first one was titled, "The G. A. P." Munson graduated from O. D. Wyatt High School and attended Texas Southern University. He opened his first business when he was 21 years old named, "V. I. P. Shoe Shine and Grocery." Writing was and still is his main outlet. He says when no one else wants to hear him, the paper always listens. Phroze has hosted many open mics and still performs at open mics every week. He has been a guest speaker at various venues. He has recorded three albums and one audio book and working on the second one of course. Phroze also does personalized greeting cards and a host of other ways to express your feelings through poetry. I hope you enjoy and thank you in advance.

Acknowledgements

First and foremost, I would like to thank God for creating me to continue creating. I would like to acknowledge my queen, "Angela" for being there for me. She keeps me going behind the scenes. I salute both of my daughters, "Ale'gna' and Serenity" for enduring having to listen to my poetry so many times riding in the car. I acknowledge my father for the example of being a speaker and my late mother for showing me this poetry thing before I knew it would become my thing. I celebrate my brothers and sister, "Ra Tem, Les, and Sharolynne" for giving me a better sibling relationship than I see with others. I would like to acknowledge A. J. Houston for being my publisher. I also want to thank Devie Perry for the cover design and every thing else she has done for me. A special shout goes to "Big Dank" for helping me with my projects. Last but not least, I would like to acknowledge you for all your support. Thank you. Your donations help take care of the people I love.

Contact information:

Facebook: Paul Phroze Munson

Instagram: phrozethegreat

E-mail: mrpauldmunson@att.net

Website: poetryyoudig.com

Love Is A Gamble

But Still Try To Win

Love Is A Gamble